Earth

CHERRY LAKE PRESS

Published in the United States of America by Cherry Lake Publishing
Ann Arbor, Michigan
www.cherrylakepublishing.com

Reading Adviser: Marla Conn, MS, Ed, Literacy specialist, Read-Ability, Inc.
Book Designer: Jennifer Wahi
Illustrator: Jeff Bane

Photo Credits: ©Triff/Shutterstock, 5; ©Aphelleon/Shutterstock, 7; ©AppleZoomZoom/Shutterstock, 9;
©My September/Shutterstock, 11; ©Andrey Prokhorov/Shutterstock, 13; ©PIA00130/NASA, p.15; ©Vladi333/
Shutterstock, 17; ©Rost9/Shutterstock, 19; ©Amanda Carden/Shutterstock, 21; ©lovelyday12/Shutterstock, 23;
Cover, 2-3, 6, 14, 22, Jeff Bane; Various vector images throughout courtesy of Shutterstock.com/

Library of Congress Cataloging-in-Publication Data

Names: Devera, Czeena, author. | Bane, Jeff, 1957- illustrator. | Devera,
  Czeena. My guide to the planets.
Title: Earth / by Czeena Devera ; illustrated by Jeff Bane.
Description: Ann Arbor, Michigan : Cherry Lake Publishing, [2020] | Series:
  My guide to the planets | Includes index. | Audience: K-1.
Identifiers: LCCN 2019030750 (print) | LCCN 2019030751 (ebook) | ISBN
  9781534158818 (hardcover) | ISBN 9781534161115 (paperback) | ISBN
  9781534162266 (ebook) | ISBN 9781534159969 (pdf)
Subjects: LCSH: Earth (Planet)--Juvenile literature.
Classification: LCC QB631.4 D46 2020 (print) | LCC QB631.4 (ebook) | DDC
  525--dc23
LC record available at https://lccn.loc.gov/2019030750
LC ebook record available at https://lccn.loc.gov/2019030751

Printed in the United States of America
Corporate Graphics

About the author: Czeena Devera grew up in the red-hot heat of Arizona surrounded by books. Her childhood bedroom had built-in bookshelves that were always full. She now lives in Michigan with an even bigger library of books.

About the illustrator: Jeff Bane and his two business partners own a studio along the American River in Folsom, California, home of the 1849 Gold Rush. When Jeff's not sketching or illustrating for clients, he's either swimming or kayaking in the river to relax.

I'm Earth. I am about 4.5 billion years old.

I am the third-closest planet to the Sun.

I am the fifth-largest planet.

I **orbit** around the Sun. It takes me about 365 days to complete 1 orbit. That's 1 year!

In 1 year, I go through different **seasons**.

While I orbit the Sun, I also spin. This is why there is night and day.

I have one moon. Without the Moon, the **climate** would be more extreme.

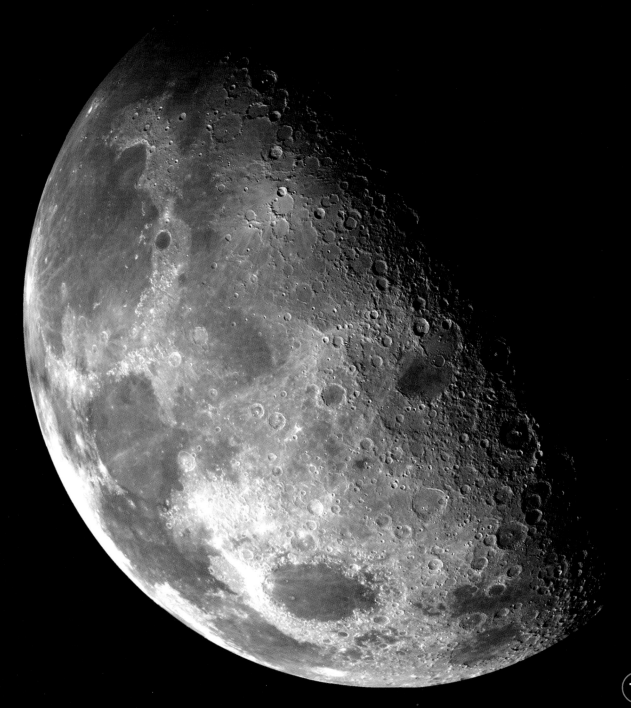

I am made up of four layers.
My top layer is the **crust**.
The oceans and land make
up the crust.

Under the crust is the **mantle**.
The mantle is made up of different
types of rocks.

My third and fourth layers are the outer and inner **cores**. It's very hot in there! My inner core is almost as hot as the Sun!

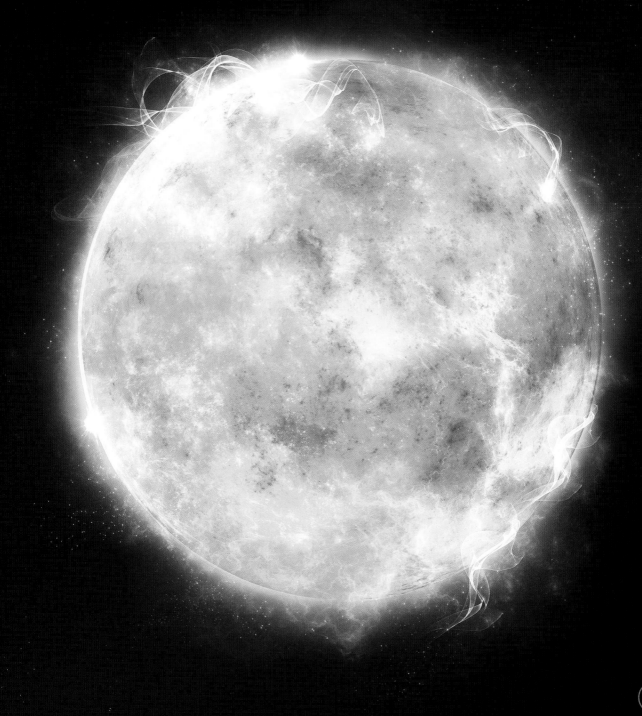

I am a **unique** planet. I am the only planet in our **solar system** that has life.

glossary

climate (KLYE-mit) the weather typical of a place over a long period of time

cores (KORZ) the very hot, most inner parts of Earth

crust (KRUHST) the hard outer layer of Earth

mantle (MAN-tuhl) the part of Earth between the crust and the core

orbit (OR-bit) to travel in a curved path around something

seasons (SEE-zuhnz) the four natural parts of the year

solar system (SOH-lur SIS-tuhm) the Sun and all the things that orbit around it, like planets

unique (yoo-NEEK) the only one of its kind

index